DATE DUE

FEB 1 4 2006	
FEB 1 4 2006	
FEB 1 4 2006	

VIETNAM
the culture

Bobbie Kalman

The Lands, Peoples, and Cultures Series

Crabtree Publishing Company

The Lands, Peoples, and Cultures Series

Created by Bobbie Kalman

For Caroline and Paul

Editor-in-Chief
Bobbie Kalman

Writing team
Bobbie Kalman
Greg Nickles
Niki Walker

Text and photo research
David Schimpky

Managing editor
Lynda Hale

Editors
Greg Nickles
Niki Walker
Virginia Mainprize
Janine Schaub

Consultant
Nancy Tingley, Wattis Curator
of Southeast Asian Art, Asian Art
Museum of San Francisco

Computer design
Lynda Hale
Greg Nickles

Special thanks to
Marc Crabtree, who, during a recent assignment in Vietnam, took
photographs that gave an accurate portrayal of modern Vietnam;
Lance Woodruff

Photographs
Jeffrey Alford/Asia Access: page 23
Jeanette Andrews-Bertheau: page 12
Marc Crabtree: cover, title page, pages 4, 5 (top & bottom),
    6-7, 7 (top left, bottom right), 10-11 (both), 13 (all), 16 (top right),
    18 (middle & bottom), 19, 20, 21 (bottom), 22, 24, 25 (bottom),
    26 (both), 28, 29 (both), 30
Naomi Duguid/Asia Access: page 14
Wolfgang Kaehler: pages 16 (top left, bottom left & right),
    21 (top), 25 (top)
Michael McDonell: pages 8 (both), 9
Tran Viet Anh: page 18 (top)
Yale University Library: pages 5 (middle), 7 (top right)

Illustrations
Barb Bedell: back cover

Separations and film
Dot 'n Line Image Inc.

Printer
Worzalla Publishing Company

The interior of the Cao Dai Great Temple is shown on the cover.
The title page shows two worshippers at the temple. The bird on the
back cover is a sarus crane, which symbolizes loyalty and long life.

Published by
Crabtree Publishing Company

350 Fifth Avenue	360 York Road, RR 4,	73 Lime Walk
Suite 3308	Niagara-on-the-Lake,	Headington
New York	Ontario, Canada	Oxford OX3 7AD
N.Y. 10118	L0S 1J0	United Kingdom

Cataloging in Publication Data
Kalman, Bobbie, 1947-
    Vietnam: the culture

(Lands, peoples, and cultures series)
Includes index.
ISBN 0-86505-225-5 (library bound) ISBN 0-86505-305-7 (pbk.)
This book looks at aspects of ancient and modern culture in
Vietnam, including music, theater, religion, architecture, clothing,
and festivals.
1. Vietnam - Social life and customs - Juvenile literature. 2. Vietnam -
Civilization - Juvenile literature. I. Title II. Series.

DS556.42.K35 1996   j959.7   LC 95-51995
                                                      CIP

Contents

Yesterday and today

When we talk about a country's culture, we are referring to the ways the people of that country express themselves. People express themselves through their clothing, the music they enjoy, the dances they perform, the food they eat, and the art they create. Culture also includes stories, plays, customs, festivals, architecture, and religious traditions. Even the way people celebrate birth and honor death are expressions of their culture.

Cultures that influenced Vietnam

Vietnam's culture reaches back to the Viet people who settled in northern Vietnam over two thousand years ago. Although many of today's customs and traditions are uniquely Vietnamese, several important features of the culture came from other places. Throughout Vietnam's long history, foreign peoples introduced their way of life and customs into Vietnamese culture.

The Chinese ruled Vietnam for hundreds of years and had a great influence on its culture. The Vietnamese began following Chinese religions and used Chinese writing symbols and medical practices. Through trade, India and the once-powerful Cham and Khmer peoples also influenced Vietnamese society. French rulers brought their European beliefs and customs. During the war between North and South Vietnam, Americans also introduced their way of life to the Vietnamese.

Opening to the world

For a number of years, the Vietnamese were not allowed to trade with most of the outside world. Gradually, however, the country is opening to foreigners who have introduced the Vietnamese to modern fashions, rock music, and fast food. Although this new way of life may become part of everyday culture, Vietnamese families still cherish their old traditions.

(top) Ruins of Cham towers, once part of the kingdom of Champa, stand in southern and central Vietnam.
(middle) The Chinese influence on Vietnamese art can be seen in this painting.
(bottom) French bread, called **baguette,** *is sold in many markets.*
(opposite page) Many young people now wear North American and European fashions.

5

Music

Most Vietnamese music is sung, and singers are often accompanied by traditional instruments. The Vietnamese have adapted several musical styles to suit their taste. The Chinese musical tradition, which is based on five **tones**, or notes, has had the greatest influence on Vietnamese musicians. More recently, classical music from Europe and rock music from China and North America have become popular. In cities today, it is not unusual to hear different kinds of music coming from discotheques, dance halls, and open-air concerts. Music is also a major part of Vietnamese theater and dance.

Instruments

A wide range of sounds can be created with Vietnamese instruments. The **zither**, a stringed instrument resembling an autoharp, is plucked and bowed to make either sharp or wailing tones. The *dan bau*, a popular single-stringed zither, can sound like a human voice. Flutes create airy, fluid notes. They are made from bamboo, a thick, woody grass that grows abundantly in Vietnam. **Percussion** instruments, such as xylophones, drums, and bells, produce gentle, pounding, and clanging sounds. Drums are especially important in classical theater, where they are played to create different moods.

Songs for work and play

Many Vietnamese songs are based on poetry and traditional folk tales. These poetic songs, called *hat a dao*, are about love and sadness. There are also boating songs, fishing songs, and songs workers sing to help them through long days of hard labor.

Songs are also a part of play and celebration. *Trong quan* or *quan ho* songs are sung by children at some village festivals. First, boys gather and sing a challenge to girls. The girls then sing a reply to the boys. The singers invent several more verses before their song is finished.

Ceremonial music

Music is a powerful part of Vietnamese ceremonies. Weddings, funerals, and special holidays are celebrated with singers and musicians. Music is important in religious life and is often heard in temples. Some worshippers recite words in a low voice, as if they are chanting. Others sing their prayers in different tones. Sometimes chants are accompanied by instruments such as drums, bells, fiddles, gongs, and cymbals.

Traditional Vietnamese musical instruments include drums, bells, zithers, and a long-handled guitar. The girl in red below is playing a **dan bau** zither.

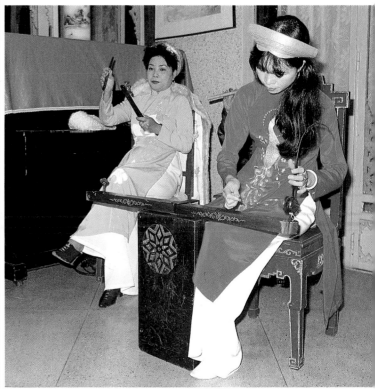

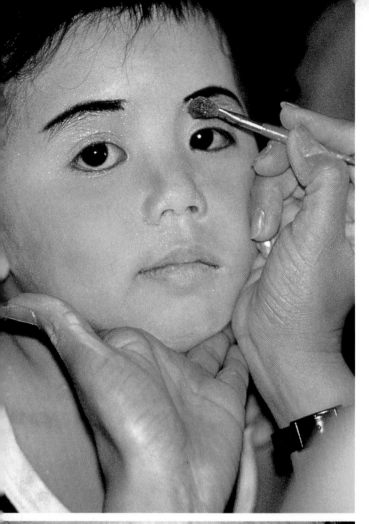

Theater is strictly controlled by Vietnam's government, which employs all of the country's actors. Despite this control, Vietnamese dramas are colorful, fun events that feature bright makeup, fancy costumes, music, and dancing.

The opera

Hat tuong is a traditional form of theater that was adapted from Chinese opera by the Vietnamese. In an opera, the actors sing their lines rather than speak them. The stories of *hat tuong* are based on myths and legends. Although the actors may seem very stiff and unnatural, theirs is a challenging style of acting that requires years of training. Audiences can recognize characters by their costumes, makeup, and gestures, which are the same in each performance. Makeup is used to show the traits of a character. For example, gold makeup signifies a god, whereas black means that a character is brave.

Playing for laughs

Hat cheo theater is a comical version of opera. It tells traditional stories in a lighthearted way. It features funny scenes, folk songs, and dance and pokes fun at the government and Vietnamese society.

Cai luong theater has been extremely popular since it was invented in the 1920s. Many **troupes**, or groups of actors, specialize in this kind of comedy. Some Westerners compare *cai luong* shows to musicals because they have many songs and dances. Surprisingly, all of the songs in *cai luong* theater have developed from one traditional love song called Vong Co. Its melody can be heard throughout any performance.

These actors belong to a **cai luong** *theater troupe. Children sometimes perform in these musical plays.*

Puppet shows

In North America, many people think of puppets as toys for children but, in Vietnam, puppetry is enjoyed by young and old. This theater art has been popular for centuries. Puppet makers and puppeteers are skilled and respected artists who spend years perfecting their talents.

Water puppets

One popular form of puppetry is called *roi nuoc*, or water puppetry. Water puppetry is unique because its "stage" is a small pond. It is said that this art was invented centuries ago when an ordinary puppet show was interrupted by one of Vietnam's many floods! From behind a backdrop, puppeteers move strings, wires, and bamboo poles to make the wooden puppets glide around on the water. The audience, sitting on the shore, often laughs at their funny tales and antics.

Shadow puppets

This traditional art uses shadows to enact ancient stories of adventure. Flat puppets are cut from pieces of leather in the shapes of characters such as princes, princesses, peasants, demons, and monkeys. The stories are told by a narrator and accompanied by musicians who set the mood for each scene.

When evening comes, a fire is lit behind a large screen of white cloth. Music begins to play. While the narrator tells the story, the puppeteers cast fantastic shadows by holding their puppets behind the screen. The shadows dance and seem to come alive before the eyes of the audience, which sits in front of the screen. In a traditional shadow puppet show, an entire story stretches over seven nights!

Water puppeteers stand waist-deep in water, hidden behind a backdrop called a puppet house.

Water puppets are carved from wood and painted by skillful artisans.

Vietnamese fashion

Today, more Vietnamese are dressing as people do in North America and Europe. The young wear jeans and T-shirts, some girls wear dresses, and business people wear suits. Traditional Vietnamese outfits are still worn, but mainly in the country and during festivals.

The *ao dai*

In the past, both men and women wore the *ao dai*. Today, it is usually worn by women. The *ao dai* is a long blouse that resembles a dress. It has long sleeves, a short collar, and slits up the sides. It is usually worn over baggy pants. The light cloth from which an *ao dai* is made can be white, black, or brightly colored.

Protection from the sun

The cone-shaped hats worn by farm workers are a common sight throughout Vietnam. These hats, called *non la*, are made of woven palm leaves.

Non la are worn to protect the face and neck from the hot tropical sun. In Vietnam, it is fashionable for women to have pale skin, so some women carry umbrellas and wear long gloves up to their elbows to avoid getting suntanned.

The value of dry feet

When shoes and boots get wet, they trap moisture, which can lead to foot diseases. Since Vietnam receives heavy rain showers during the summer, most people wear sandals. Feet can dry quickly in these open shoes.

Clothes in the north

In northern Vietnam, where the weather is cooler, people dress in warm clothing. The black or dark blue fabric of the hill tribes is often decorated with beautiful embroidery. Silver jewelry, beads, and pompoms are special adornments. Sometimes clothes are decorated with old coins!

(top) These young women are wearing the traditional ao dai.
(right) This northern hill-tribe woman wears a brightly colored scarf over her dark blue clothing.
(bottom) In rural areas, most people wear loose clothing that allows them to move and work easily.
(opposite page) Cone-shaped hats keep farmers from getting sunburned.

Flavors of the land and sea

Vietnamese food is known around the world for its many spices and flavors. It is cooked on a clay or brick stove heated with charcoal or wood. In the city, the streets are fragrant with the smell of food cooking on portable stoves set up at food stands. Fresh vegetables are bought every day at the market because few people have refrigerators. Rice and vegetables are part of every meal. Pork is a more popular meat than chicken or beef, and duck is saved for special occasions. Shrimp is a favorite seafood.

An important grain

Rice is Vietnam's most important crop. Some of it is eaten by the people of Vietnam, and the rest is sold to other countries. Rice, in different forms, is a part of almost every meal. The kernels of the rice plant can be boiled until the rice is light and fluffy. Sometimes the rice kernels are ground up into flour and used to make thin noodles. Rice flour is also made into rice paper, a thin sheet in which meat and vegetables are wrapped before they are eaten.

Eating Vietnamese-style

For each meal, a family gathers around a low table or, in the country, around a straw mat. Rice is served in individual bowls, but vegetables and meat are served in communal dishes. People use their own chopsticks to serve themselves.

Fish sauce

Fish sauce is part of most meals. It is made from salted anchovies, which are fermented in a vat for months. *Nuoc cham* is a diluted form of the sauce. Many foods are dipped in *nuoc cham*. It is made with equal parts of fish sauce and water. Vinegar, garlic, sugar, and chili are added for extra flavor.

Finger food

When you eat Vietnamese spring rolls, it is not impolite to use your fingers—in fact, it is necessary. Spring rolls are made of seafood, meat, vegetables, and egg, wrapped in noodle dough and fried to a crispy brown. The fried spring roll is rolled up in a leaf of lettuce along with mint, cucumber, and shredded carrot. It is then dipped in *nuoc cham*. This tasty treat can be eaten as an appetizer or a snack.

Wake up! Soup's on!

Pho is a noodle soup that is enjoyed at any time of the day, but most people eat it for breakfast. If you want to try this tasty soup, you might want to wait until lunch. It can be very filling! When cooking, make sure that an adult is present to help you use a knife and the stove.

Ingredients:
100 g (4 ounces) of vermicelli or rice noodles
85 g (3 ounces) of beef (sliced thin)
750 ml (3 cups) beef broth
2 medium onions (diced)
30 ml (2 tablespoons) fish sauce
8 ml (1/2 tablespoon) vinegar
15 ml (1 tablespoon) minced ginger
2.5 ml (1/2 teaspoon) salt

Bring broth to a boil and add onion, ginger, salt, vinegar, and fish sauce. Simmer for ten minutes. Add noodles and boil until they are soft.

Add the beef, then simmer for one minute. Remove the soup from heat. Garnish with basil, chili peppers, and fresh mint for extra flavor.

French fare

When the French controlled Vietnam, they introduced their breads and pastries to the country. Today, stands selling *baguettes*, *croissants*, and french pastries are found in many markets. The Vietnamese also cook *crêpes*, which are very thin pancakes.

Sweet delights

Vietnamese desserts usually consist of beans, fruit, and sweet, sticky rice, wrapped up in leaves. Coconuts and bananas, which grow in the south, are used in many desserts. One popular dessert is fried bananas. Try them with ice cream or pour honey on them.

Ingredients:
2 large, firm bananas (sliced lengthwise into 3 pieces)
65 ml (1/4 cup) milk
1 egg
15 ml (1 tablespoon) brown sugar
125 ml (1/2 cup) flour
icing sugar
vegetable or peanut oil for frying

Mix together milk, egg, sugar, and flour. Pour the mixture into a shallow bowl and dip the bananas into it. Ask an adult to heat a pan and pour in some oil. When the oil is hot, place the bananas in the pan, using tongs. Remove the bananas when they turn brown. Place them on a paper towel to cool. Sprinkle with icing sugar and serve.

(opposite page) This tasty shrimp dish was prepared by a vendor on a city street. Seafood, an important part of the Vietnamese diet, is served throughout the country. Some restaurants also feature unusual dishes, such as cobra, bat, and lizard meat!

Architecture

Many different peoples and cultures have been involved in Vietnam's history. Traces of their influence on Vietnam's culture can be seen in the country's remarkable variety of building styles, or **architecture**.

Cham structures
From AD 100 to 1600, the coast of central Vietnam was part of a kingdom called Champa. The Cham people built cities with palaces, temples, and homes. Over the centuries, most of these buildings were reduced to ruins, but some of the temples still stand. These red brick structures look like tall, narrow towers. Most have three stories, or levels, each one smaller than the one beneath. Detailed sculptures decorate the inside and outside of these temples.

Pagodas
Some of the most elaborate buildings in Vietnam are the Chinese-style temples called **pagodas**. They are decorated with sculptures and painted wood. The inside of a pagoda reflects the blending of different faiths in Vietnam. Statues of Buddha, the founder of Buddhism, and **bodhisattvas**, Buddhist holy people, are found in and around pagodas. Most pagodas also have a statue of the Jade Emperor, the ruler of all gods in the Taoist religion.

The Hué Citadel
In the early 1800s, Emperor Gia Long ordered the construction of a huge **citadel**, or walled fortress, in the city of Hué. It took thousands of artisans and laborers many years to complete this enormous project. The Citadel's design was based on the huge Forbidden City in Beijing, China. Architects designed the Citadel to be a strong fortress as well as a magnificent residence for Vietnamese emperors.

Three cities in one
Inside the Citadel's thick outer wall, a second wall, the Imperial Enclosure, was built. It surrounded the Forbidden Purple City, which was the emperor's residence. These two walls not only doubled Hué's protection from invaders, they also divided Hué into three small "cities."

Artisans and merchants lived in the first city, which was just inside the outer wall. The second city was between the inner wall and the Forbidden Purple City. It had many temples and libraries and was home to court officials and Buddhist monks. The Forbidden Purple City was open only to the emperor, his family, and his closest advisors.

French architecture
When the French ruled Vietnam as a colony, they constructed many buildings in major cities such as Hanoi, Da Nang, and Ho Chi Minh City. These cities were the centers of government for the colony, and the impressive buildings were a display of French power.

Today, these beautiful French-style buildings still line the wide boulevards of large cities. Shuttered windows, intricate ironwork, and pastel yellow colors are among the features of French colonial architecture. The French also built churches and cathedrals so that European and Vietnamese Catholics would have places for worship.

opposite page:
(top left) A beautifully decorated Cham tower stands in ruins.
(top right) The French influenced the architecture of many buildings in Hanoi and Ho Chi Minh City.
(bottom left) Both the inside and outside of Buddhist pagodas are elaborately decorated with carvings and statues.
(bottom right) The tomb of the emperor Khai Dinh is in the former imperial city of Hué.

(top) Using many colors of thread, skilled weavers create complicated designs in their fabrics.
(right) The inside of the cone-shaped non-la hat is ribbed to give it shape and strength.
(bottom) This fantastic dragon boat and the laughing Buddha statue were carved from wood.

Arts and crafts

For thousands of years, Vietnamese artisans have created beautiful handicrafts. Their ancient skills have been handed down from generation to generation. Children first learn these skills by watching their parents work. When they have enough knowledge of the craft, the children begin perfecting their skills by working as apprentices to their parents.

Sometimes everyone in a village makes the same type of handicraft. In Hanoi, there is a community of artists called 36 Streets. Each street features artisans who specialize in one craft.

Ceramics

During the rule of the Chinese, from 111 BC to AD 939, Vietnamese artisans learned how to create glazed pottery, or **ceramics**. The art of making ceramics continues today. A family of artisans often has its own workshop where potters mold clay into vases, dishes, and cups. The clay items are baked in a large oven called a **kiln** until they harden and turn white. The pottery is then painted with a glaze and baked again. The kiln's intense heat melts the glaze and, as it cools, it forms a layer of colored glass over the pottery. The most famous Vietnamese ceramics are those decorated with delicate blue-and-white designs.

Working in wood

For centuries, craftspeople have carved the hardwoods of the rainforest into ornate boxes and statues. Creating **lacquerware** is another old woodworking skill. Lacquerware items, such as vases and furniture, are made of wood with inlaid designs of gold, silver, mother-of-pearl, or eggshell. Their surfaces are covered with a shiny coating of lacquer, which comes from the sap of the *son* tree. Lacquer adds to the rich colors and grains of the hardwoods and makes them shine. Artisans apply ten coats of lacquer to the wooden crafts. Each coat takes seven days to dry!

Weaving

Weaving fabric is another traditional art. Hoi An, in central Vietnam, was once a center of fine silk production. Vietnamese officials wore rich robes of silk to show their importance. European traders who visited Hoi An eagerly bought Vietnamese silk and brocades.

Many mountain peoples practice the art of weaving cloth. They create colorful blankets and clothing on traditional looms. People in the country also weave straw, grass, and rice stalks into hats, baskets, and mats.

This laquerware screen was made shiny with natural resin, or sap. Today, many artisans use artificial resins to finish their crafts.

Most of the religions now practiced in Vietnam came from other parts of the world. Taoist and Confucian beliefs were brought to Vietnam by Chinese rulers. Around AD 100, monks from neighboring countries introduced Buddhism to the Vietnamese. As a result of these influences from China and India, most people in Vietnam follow Confucian, Taoist, and Buddhist beliefs. Belief in a combination of these three religions is called Tam Giao, or Triple Religion.

Confucianism

Confucius was a Chinese teacher who lived long ago. He taught people to honor their parents, government leaders, and teachers. He believed that education was very important. His ideas still play a strong role in Vietnamese beliefs.

Christianity

When Europeans began traveling to Vietnam in the 1600s, missionaries came to spread Roman Catholicism, which is a Christian faith. Christians follow the lessons of Jesus. Many people became Catholic even though they were punished by the emperors, who were against the teachings of the missionaries. Roman Catholicism spread during French rule, and today one in ten Vietnamese is Christian.

Mahayana Buddhism

Most Vietnamese are Buddhists. Buddhists believe that each person lives many lives. The cycle of living and dying ends only when a person reaches **nirvana**, or ultimate peace. Buddhists believe that a great teacher named Gautama Buddha reached nirvana through meditation.

The Vietnamese practice a form of Buddhism called Mahayana Buddhism, which is the main religion of Vietnam. Its followers believe that worldly things are not important. Living saints, who have reached nirvana, are called bodhisattvas. They show patience and compassion toward others and help them reach nirvana. Buddhists offer prayers to these holy people.

Taoism

Taoism, pronounced "dowism," also came to Vietnam from China. People believe that Lao Tse started this religion and wrote a short book called Tao Te Ching. Lao Tse taught that the way to find peace is to live a simple life in harmony with nature.

In Vietnam, the Taoist religion is centered around the Jade Emperor, who is the ruler over all the gods.

Taoists believe that there is a universal force present in all things. The symbol of this force is the yin yang circle, which is called *am duong* in Vietnamese. The black and white halves of the circle symbolize that opposite things, such as good and evil, hot and cold, and sweet and sour, exist together. When these opposites are in balance, the body and soul are at peace.

The yin and yang contain parts of each other.

(top) Worshippers pray in front of the statues of Buddha in this temple.
(right) Taoists offer burning incense in memory of the dead.
(opposite page) At the Jade Pagoda, sticks of incense burn in front of the statue of the Jade Emperor.

Cao Dai

The Cao Dai faith originated in Vietnam. More than two million people follow this religion. They believe in one God, who has a female counterpart called the Mother Goddess.

The followers of Cao Dai accept the lessons of Muhammad, Jesus, Buddha, and many other teachers. The center of the Cao Dai faith is a large temple in the town of Long Hoa, near Ho Chi Minh City.

Ancestor worship

The worship of ancestors is an important part of Confucian and Taoist beliefs. People believe that the soul lives on after death and remains on earth to protect its descendants. The Vietnamese honor their dead relatives regularly, especially on the anniversary of their death. Most homes have altars where people can pray and make offerings to their ancestors. They believe that, in return, the spirits of their ancestors will help them achieve success in school or in business.

Good and bad luck

Some Vietnamese believe that much of their good or bad fortune is a matter of luck. They consult the stars and constantly watch for signs that will give them clues about their future. They even hire experts to tell them how to build and furnish their houses. A properly built home is supposed to assure prosperity and good luck.

Watching the stars

Astrology is the belief that the stars affect people's lives and can show the future. In Vietnam and other Asian countries, a person's date of birth is very important because, according to astrology, it decides his or her character and destiny. Experts in astrology, called **astrologers**, are consulted to foretell a person's future based on his or her date of birth. Some people make important decisions based on these predictions.

It could be your lucky day!

Many Vietnamese believe that countless things influence luck. For example, the number nine is very lucky. Seeing a bat or passing a funeral also means good luck is on its way. Seeing chopsticks stand upright in a bowl of rice, though, could mean that a death is in the near future. The chopsticks remind people of incense sticks, which are burned for ancestors in the temples.

(above) These women are carrying offerings of food to the temple.

 # A monk's life

Most Vietnamese cities, towns, and villages have a pagoda which is the center of the community's spiritual life. Many Vietnamese follow Buddhist beliefs and contribute a portion of their earnings to support the monks who look after pagodas.

Monks are Buddhist men who devote their entire lives to their religion. In some countries, Buddhist monks live apart in their own religious communities. In Vietnam, they have important and active roles in community life.

Becoming a monk

If a boy wishes to become a monk, he applies to a regional Buddhist center, which then assigns him to a pagoda. There, he will live, study, and work with other monks.

Monks wear robes and keep their hair very short. Their everyday robes are gray or brown, but they dress in yellow robes for special occasions. Monks cannot own anything, so they must rely on the people who visit the pagoda to give them food and other necessary supplies.

Different levels

There are several different stages of becoming a monk. Beginner monks are called **novices**. After a monk turns twenty, he can write a difficult exam on Buddhist beliefs. If he passes, he is raised to the second level. Years of further study are required before the monk is ready to write an exam to reach the third level. Monks who pass this exam are honored with the title "Thich." Even more highly honored are the few monks who reach the fourth and fifth levels.

(left) The founder of the Buddhist faith, the Buddha, is represented by the golden statue on this altar. (opposite page, top) Monks must study hard to reach their next level. These young monks are writing exams. (opposite page, bottom) These nuns, who also devote their lives to Buddhism, are preparing a meal.

Daily routine

A monk's day is very long. It begins early in the morning with prayers and the study of Buddhist teachings. At noon, it is time for the first meal of the day. Buddhist monks do not eat meat because harming animals is forbidden. They eat rice, vegetables, mushrooms, and **tofu**, a food made from soybeans. After this meal, the monks rest for a while.

In the afternoon, there is more study time. Some monks work in the community, visiting sick people or performing ceremonies in the pagoda. After dinner, there is evening prayer. Before going to bed, the monks have time to relax or go for walks. They spend the night sleeping on simple mats.

(top) This young couple has chosen a modern, western-style wedding ceremony.
(bottom) Remembering ancestors is an important tradition. Here, offerings of food and incense have been laid out at a family altar.

Family celebrations

Families enjoy celebrating special events, such as birthdays, weddings, and deaths, together. They also gather together to celebrate national holidays and festivals.

Baby's first birthday

A baby's first birthday is one of the most exciting events of childhood. Family and friends are invited to a party at which the parents officially introduce the baby with his or her given name. After this first party, a person's individual birthday is no longer celebrated. Instead, people honor their birthday on Tet, the Vietnamese new year, when everyone becomes one year older.

Wedding bells

A wedding is an exciting and joyous event for families. In the past, the marriage partners of young people were selected by their parents. Today, couples are free to choose their partners, but family approval is still necessary.

Matchmakers

An older, respected man and wife may act as **matchmakers** for a young couple. Matchmakers help arrange a wedding. They consult an astrologer to decide on the best dates for the engagement party and wedding ceremony. If the stars are in a lucky position on the days of these ceremonies, the couple is supposed to have a happy marriage.

Uniting the families

It is important for the families of the young couple to be included in the festivities because they, too, will be united by the wedding. The matchmakers arrange for the families to be officially introduced at the engagement party.

In a special ceremony, the matchmakers present the women with betel nuts and the men with rice wine. Enjoying these treats together is a traditional sign of friendship.

Gifts galore

The young couple receives many gifts at the engagement party. Some are supposed to bring the couple good luck, whereas others are objects that the couple will need to begin their life together. The groom presents his future wife with a tray of gold engagement jewelry.

Tying the knot

On the day of the ceremony, a traditional bride wears a special pink or red *ao dai*, and the groom wears a blue one. The couple stands in front of a family altar, and the matchmakers light two red candles. The bride and groom exchange rings, and their hands are tied together with a pink thread, which symbolizes their happiness. The couple then eats a piece of ginger dipped in salt. Its unpleasant taste represents the challenges the couple will face together. The matchmakers bow, announce that the couple is married, and then everyone gathers at the groom's home for a huge wedding feast.

Changing traditions

Today, many city weddings are based on North American, rather than Vietnamese, traditions. Instead of an *ao dai*, the bride wears a wedding gown, and the groom wears a suit. Some couples exchange their vows in a church rather than in front of their family altar.

Celebrating loved ones

Although the death of a relative is a sad event for Vietnamese families, it is also a time to remember and celebrate that person's life. One hundred days after the death, family members travel from afar to attend a huge feast. The relative's favorite foods are prepared and placed in front of the family altar. Before enjoying the feast, everyone bows to show their respect. A similar feast is held each year to honor the relative's departure to the spirit world.

Time for Tet!

For the Vietnamese, Tet Nguyen Dan, or Tet, is the most important festival of the year. It is the traditional new year and marks the beginning of spring. People celebrate with special parades, feasts, dances, and family gatherings. Tet is usually celebrated near the end of January or early February. In the past, Tet festivities lasted more than a week, but today the festival is officially celebrated for only three days. Workers and schoolchildren are given days off so they can enjoy the holiday.

Getting ready

Preparations begin weeks before Tet. Family is the most important part of the celebration, so people make plans to travel home for the holiday—even from overseas. Everyone pitches in to make sure the house is spotless before the guests arrive. It is especially important that the family shrine is clean because the spirits of ancestors are honored during the festival.

A flowery festival

A popular Tet custom is to decorate the house with flowers. Apricot and plum blossoms, chrysanthemums, and other fresh flowers are placed throughout homes as a symbol of the new spring. Budding branches of the *hoa moi* tree are cut and brought indoors. If they bloom before Tet begins, the family can expect to have good luck for the year.

Housekeeping reports

Another Tet tradition is to get ready for the visit of Ong Tao, the kitchen spirit. Legend says that on new year's day, Ong Tao flies from earth to the Jade Emperor, the ruler of all gods. He brings the Jade Emperor reports on each family's housekeeping. A good report brings good luck for the year, so families leave Ong Tao gifts of fruit, honey, and paper money in their kitchens. A paper fish is also left for Ong Tao so he can ride it back to the home of the gods.

The night before Tet

On the eve of Tet, families gather for a huge meal. A favorite treat is *banh chung*, a small rice cake, wrapped in banana leaves, that has sweet bean paste and pork in the center. Other special Tet foods include fried watermelon seeds, dried fruit, candy, and pickled vegetables.

Families include their ancestors in this feast by placing food on the family altar. At midnight, firecrackers explode around the country to welcome the new year and scare away evil spirits. The lunar new year begins with a bang!

Starting off right

The first day of the new year is very important because whatever happens on this day will affect the rest of the year. It is a time for visiting. To ensure good luck, each family invites a respected person to be the first visitor of the year. Special greetings, written in the ancient *chu nom* script, are sent to friends and neighbors. To start the year off right, people wear new clothes, repay debts, and settle arguments. If children were well-behaved in the previous year, they receive gifts of money wrapped in red rice paper.

(opposite page) Flowers symbolize the new year, new growth, and the coming of spring.
(top) Happy New Year balloons can be seen everywhere during Tet.
(above) Firecrackers scare away evil spirits.

A year of festivals

Besides Tet, the Vietnamese have many other festivals throughout the year to celebrate religious feasts, ancestors, and the changing of the seasons. Firecrackers, colorful lanterns, fresh flowers, delicious foods, and sweet-smelling incense are often part of the festivities.

Watch the moon

Today, most people use a solar calendar which has 365 days in each year. This calendar measures the length of time it takes the earth to orbit once around the sun. In the past, the Vietnamese followed a lunar calendar. It was based on the cycles of the moon and had 355 days in each year. This lunar calendar is still used to calculate the dates of traditional Vietnamese holidays.

Holidays for the dead

The Doan Ngu festival marks the longest day of the year—the summer solstice. It occurs on the fifth day of the fifth lunar month. On this solemn day, paper **effigies** are burned as offerings to the god of death to appease him and prevent the spread of diseases.

The fifteenth day of the seventh lunar month is the beginning of Trung Nguyen, which lasts for a month. It is believed that during this time the souls of the dead wander the earth. People make offerings of food and incense to their ancestors to give them comfort during their travels.

Harvest moon

On the fifteenth day of the eighth lunar month, the mid-autumn festival, or Tet Trung-thu, is held to celebrate the harvest. This festival is also called the Moon Festival because the full moon is largest and brightest at this time of year.

Children celebrate Tet Trung-thu by making rice-paper lanterns, which are hung on long bamboo poles. Some lanterns are shaped like stars or fish, and others are covered in fancy designs. After dark, the candles inside the lanterns are lit, and the children march in a colorful parade. They carefully protect their lanterns from the wind. To reach the end of the parade without the lantern catching fire is a real challenge!

After the parade, children return home to a special treat of **moon cakes**, made with rice, peanuts, raisins, watermelon seeds, and eggs.

Honoring heroes

Many towns and villages hold festivals to celebrate the heroes in Vietnam's history. In some festivals, people dress in historical costumes. The Trung Sisters Festival is one such celebration. It is held to honor the two women who overthrew the Chinese rulers in AD 39. Each town and village chooses two girls to dress up in colorful costumes like those worn by the sisters. The girls ride through the streets, reminding people of the important contributions women have made in Vietnam's history.

3 4 5 6 7 8 9 0 Printed in the USA 5 4 3 2 1 0 9 8 7

🧘 Glossary 🧘

adornment A decoration

altar A place where religious ceremonies are performed or offerings are made in worship

ancestor A person from whom one is descended

apprentice A person who works for an artisan in order to learn an art or craft

architecture The art, design, and construction of buildings or structures

artisan A person who is skilled in a craft

astrology The study of the position of the stars and planets and their influence on people's lives

backdrop A painted scene at the back of a stage

betel nut A seed which sweetens the breath when chewed and turns saliva red

boulevard A wide city street lined with trees

brocade A shiny fabric with a rich, raised, woven design

ceramic Pottery that has been glazed and baked at very high temperatures

Cham Describing the culture and people associated with the former kingdom of Champa, which was in central Vietnam

citadel A fort

colonial Describing a land or people ruled by another country

counterpart One that closely resembles and balances another

culture The customs, beliefs, and arts of a group of people

custom A practice followed by a person or group

descendant Someone who is an offspring of another person

effigy An image of a hated person; effigies are usually burned

embroidery The act or art of decorating cloth with needlework

hill tribe A group of people that lives in Vietnam's highlands and has its own culture

incense Wood or resin that produces a sweet-smelling smoke when burned

ironwork Decorative things made of iron, such as railings, fences, and balconies

Khmer Describing the culture and people associated with a former empire based in what is now Cambodia and southern Vietnam

lacquerware Objects made of wood, coated with a shiny resin

lunar Relating to the moon

matchmaker A person who brings couples together and arranges marriages

monk A man who devotes his life to religion and lives in a monastery

myth A traditional story, not usually true, that tells the beliefs of a group of people

narrator A person who tells a story

novice Someone who has entered a religious order and has not yet taken his or her final vows

nun A woman who devotes her life to a religion

pagoda A temple that is usually tower-shaped and found in eastern countries. Some pagodas look like several one-story buildings piled on top of one another.

percussion Relating to musical instruments that are played by striking

saint A person recognized by a religious faith for his or her goodness or service to others

solar Relating to the sun

solstice Either of two times in the year when the sun appears farthest from the equator

temple A place of worship

tofu A food made from soybeans

traditional Describing customs that are handed down from one generation to another

universal Relating to or affecting the whole world and universe

western Relating to countries of the western part of the world, such as the United States or France

zither A musical instrument with one or many strings that are stretched over a stick, bar, or flat box

DATE DUE			